How We Use

Metal

Chris Oxlade

www.raintreepublishers.co.uk

Visit our website to find out more information about **Raintree** books.

To order:
- ☎ Phone 44 (0) 1865 888112
- 🗎 Send a fax to 44 (0) 1865 314091
- 🖥 Visit the Raintree bookshop at **www.raintreepublishers.co.uk** to browse our catalogue and order online.

First published in Great Britain by Raintree, Halley Court, Jordan Hill, Oxford OX2 8EJ, part of Harcourt Education.
Raintree is a registered trademark of Harcourt Education Ltd.

Editorial: Nicholas Hunter and Richard Woodham
Design: Kim Saar and Bridge Creative Services Ltd
Picture Research: Maria Joannou and Debra Weatherley
Production: Amanda Meaden
Indexing: Indexing Specialists (UK) Ltd

Originated by Ambassador Litho Ltd
Printed and bound in Hong Kong, China by South China Printing Company

ISBN 1 844 43436 2
09 08 07 06 05
10 9 8 7 6 5 4 3 2 1

British Library Cataloguing in Publication Data
Oxlade, Chris
How We Use Metals. – (Using Materials)
620.1'6
A full catalogue record for this book is available from the British Library.

Acknowledgements
The publishers would like to thank the following for permission to reproduce photographs: Alamy p. 20; Art Directors pp. 8 (Trip/David Tarrant), 9 (Trip/Martin Barlow), 25 (Trip/John Wender); Corbis pp. 7 (Harcourt Index), 14 (Owaki-Kulla), 19 (Harcourt Education Ltd.), 22 (Harcourt Education Ltd.), 24 (George Diebold), 27 (Owen Franken); Ecoscene p. 18; photolibrary.com p. 23; Science Photo Library pp. 5 (Maximilian Stock Ltd), 6 (Publiphoto Diffusion/P. G. Adam), 10 (Pascal Goetgheluk), 11 (Tek Image), 12 (Alex Bartel), 13 (Tony Craddock), 15 (Tek Image), 16 (Andrew Syred), 21 (Adrienne Hart-Davis), 28 (John Mead), 29 (John Mead); Trevor Clifford p. 17; Trip p. 4 (H. Rogers); Tudor Photography p. 26.

Cover photograph of metal ventilation pipes in a factory, reproduced with permission of Getty Images.

Every effort has been made to contact copyright holders of any material reproduced in this book. Any omissions will be rectified in subsequent printings if notice is given to the publishers.

The paper used to print this book comes from sustainable resources.

Contents

Any words appearing in bold, **like this**, are explained in the Glossary.

Metals and their properties

All the things we use are made from materials. Metals are materials. There are many different types of metal. We use metals for thousands of different jobs. Metals are used to make engines and huge buildings. Metal nuts and bolts join things together. Some metals are used to make beautiful jewellery.

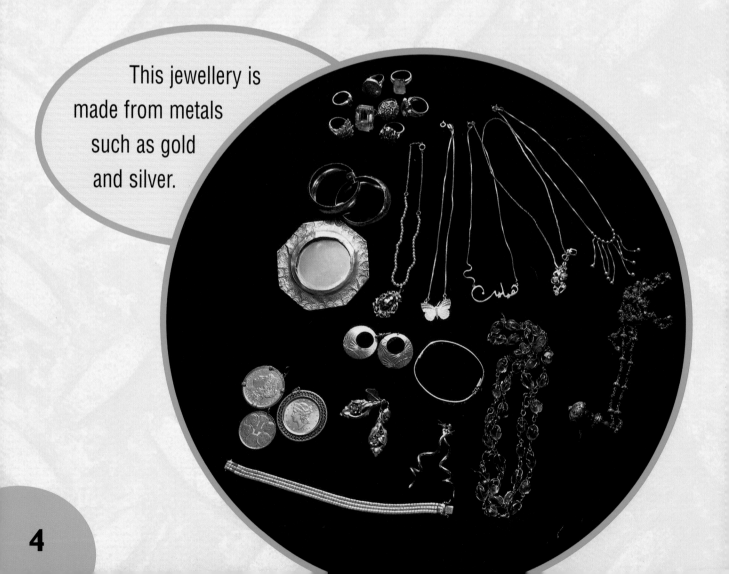

This jewellery is made from metals such as gold and silver.

Huge pieces of metal are used to build a ship.

The **properties** of a material tell us what it is like. One property of many metals is that they are hard and strong. Most metals must be heated to a very high **temperature** before they melt. All metals are shiny. They all **conduct** electricity and heat. Some metals can be made into **magnets**.

Don't use it!

The different properties of materials make them useful for some jobs. The properties also make them unsuitable for other jobs. For example, sheets of metal don't bend easily, so we don't use metals for making clothes.

Where do metals come from?

Most metals come from **natural raw materials**. These raw materials are rocks from the Earth's **crust**. The rocks that contain metals are called **ores**. For example, we get aluminium from an ore called bauxite. Ores are dug from the ground at mines. Most ore mines are giant holes in the ground where the ore is broken up by explosives.

Copper ore is dug from the ground at this mine in Arizona, USA.

This molten iron has been made by smelting iron ore.

Metals are locked tightly in ores. We cannot get them out by smashing the ores up. We have to use **chemicals** and lots of heat instead. This is called **smelting**. For example, to get iron from iron ore we heat the ore to more than 1000° Celsius. **Coke** and **limestone** are added which remove the other chemicals from the ore, leaving **molten** iron.

Metals in the past

The metals people used in the past were the ones that were easiest to get from rocks. People have made things from gold for about 10,000 years because pure gold was found in lumps. Copper and tin were discovered about 6000 years ago and iron about 3000 years ago.

Metals in machines

Most metals are tough. They do not break when we squash, stretch or bend them. They are good for making things that have to be very strong. Think about a bicycle. Its frame is made from aluminium tubes and its wheels are made from **steel**.

Many metals are also very hard materials. It is difficult to mark the surface of these metals. Things made from these metals are hard-wearing and last a long time. We use hard metals to make things that will be rubbed, scraped or hit.

Machine parts such as these ball bearings are made from steel.

The metal springs on this train absorb bumps from the tracks.

Scientists say that metals are **elastic**. This means metals can stretch, squash and bend slightly and then go back into shape. We cannot normally see these movements because they are very small. We can see them in springs, which can squash and stretch a lot. We use springs in many machines and objects, from tiny ones in watches to huge ones in trucks and trains. Springs can stretch and squash thousands of times without breaking.

Metals in the home

The strength and hardness of metals makes them good materials for making tools such as hammers, spanners and screwdrivers. Kitchen knives are made from metal so that they do not snap when you cut food. We also use metals for fixings such as nuts, bolts, nails, screws, hinges and brackets.

Saw blades are also made from metal.

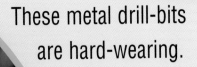

These metal drill-bits are hard-wearing.

For some jobs we need metals to be extremely hard. One way to make a metal harder is to add other metals to it to make an **alloy**. Tools such as spanners are made from an alloy that contains the metals **steel**, chromium and vanadium. It is almost impossible to scratch or dent. We also make metals harder by heating them until they are red hot and then dipping them in cold water to cool them quickly. This is called tempering.

Don't use it!
A piece of metal is heavier than a similar-sized piece of most other materials, such as plastic. This means that objects made of certain metals are very heavy. So we don't use these metals to make things that must be lightweight, such as suitcases.

Metals for building

Many buildings have **steel** frames that hold up their walls and roofs. The frame is made of **columns** and **beams**. They are joined together with steel nuts and bolts. The frame is made from a type of steel called high-tensile steel. This is much stronger than normal steel. Many bridges are also made using steel beams. A suspension bridge is held up by thick, strong steel cables.

The cables that hold up a suspension bridge are made from hundreds of thin steel wires twisted together.

Steel frames are used when constructing tall buildings.

In buildings we also use steel with **concrete**. The concrete sets around a frame of steel bars. The steel and concrete together are called reinforced concrete. It is an extremely strong material. The tallest buildings in the world are built using reinforced concrete.

Don't use it!

Not all metals are useful for building. Some metals, such as copper, are soft and bendy. We don't use them for making building frames because they are not strong enough.

13

Shaping metals

We can change the shape of a piece of metal by hammering it. For example, if you step on an empty aluminium drinks can, you can crush it. We could not do this with a material such as glass, which would shatter into pieces. A piece of metal can also be stretched to make it long and thin. For example, we can make a thin metal wire by carefully pulling a metal rod.

A blacksmith uses a hammer to shape hot metal.

Metals can be made into shapes when they are hot or cold. 'Casting' is making a metal object by pouring **molten** metal into a mould. Hammering and rolling metals into shape is easier when the metals are heated until they are red hot and soft. When metals are cold they can be cut with saws and drills. Sheets of metal can also be pressed into shapes such as baking trays and car body panels.

Joining with metal

*A weld is made by heating the edges of two pieces of metal to make them melt and join together. Solder is an **alloy** that melts easily and **conducts** electricity well. We use it to join wires together in electric circuits.*

These workers are pouring molten metal into a mould.

Metals for electricity

All metals allow electricity to flow through them. We say that they **conduct** electricity. Copper is used to make wires that carry electricity from one place to another. Copper is a soft metal, so copper wires are easy to bend round corners. We also use copper to make **circuit boards** inside computers and calculators. The thick cables that hang from electricity pylons are made from a metal called aluminium. This is because aluminium cables are light and easy for the pylons to hold up.

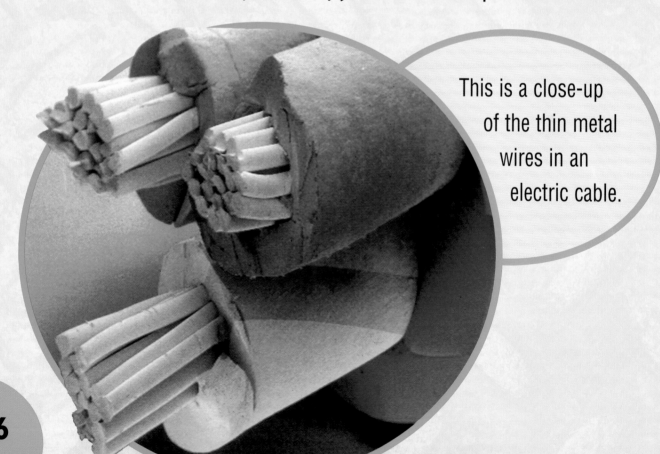

This is a close-up of the thin metal wires in an electric cable.

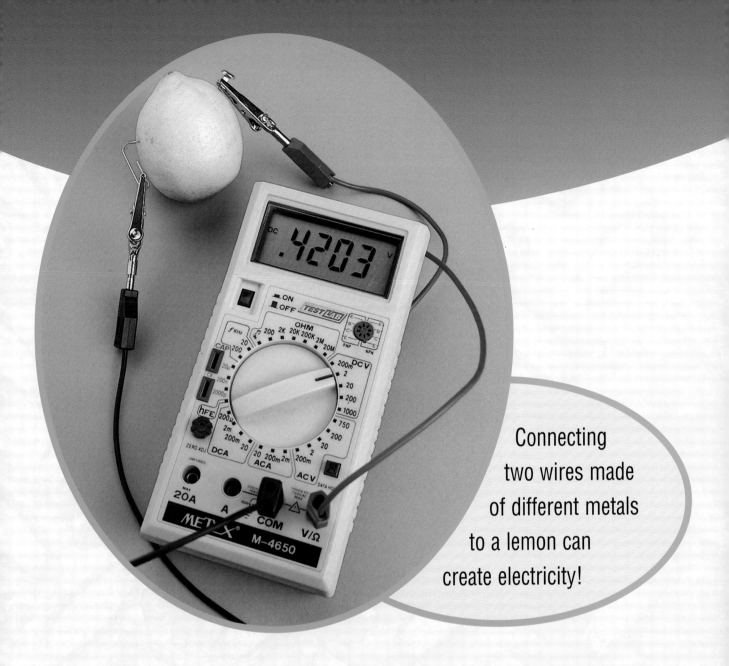

Connecting two wires made of different metals to a lemon can create electricity!

We also use metals to make electricity. Batteries always contain metals. Inside a battery, two different metals work together to make electricity. For example, a ni-cad battery contains the metals nickel and cadmium. Ni-cad batteries are **rechargeable** and are used in mobile phones and battery-powered toys.

Metals for magnets

The metals iron, cobalt and nickel are very special. They are the only metals that can be made magnetic. Things made from these metals are attracted to **magnets**. We can also make magnets from these metals.

For example, we can make an iron bar into a magnet by stroking it with another magnet.

These nails are attracted to the magnet because they contain iron.

A compass needle is made of iron or steel.

Magnets and **electromagnets** have dozens of uses. Fridge magnets are very simple. We use them to hold pieces of paper on the door of a fridge. The needle in a compass is a magnet. It always swings round to point North because the Earth works like a giant magnet. Electric motors, **dynamos** and loudspeakers contain magnets, too.

Metals and heat

Most metals only melt at high **temperatures**. That means we have to make them very hot before they turn from a **solid** to a **liquid**. This is why we use metals to make objects that get hot, such as ovens and barbecues. We also use metals to make parts of machines that get hot, such as car exhausts. Other materials, such as plastic, would melt if they were used.

The temperature of a jet engine can reach over 2800° Celsius!

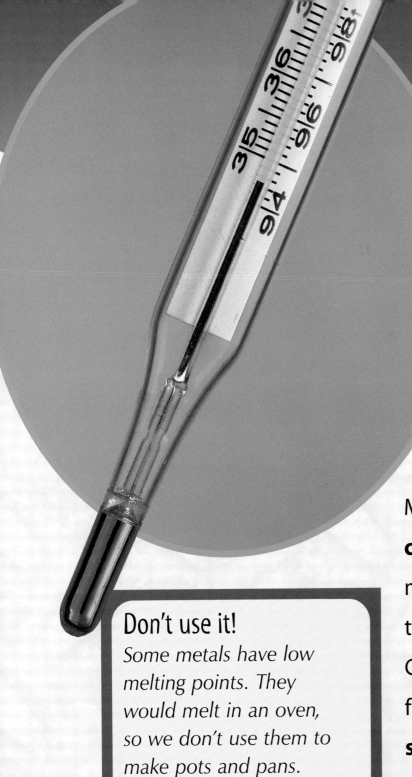

A thermometer uses mercury to show the temperature.

Metals are also good at **conducting** heat. This means that heat flows through metals well. Cooking pans are made from metals such as **steel**, aluminium and copper. Heat from the stove moves through the metal to the food in the pan.

Don't use it!

Some metals have low melting points. They would melt in an oven, so we don't use them to make pots and pans. Mercury is a peculiar metal because it is a liquid at room temperature. We have to cool it down to make it into a solid.

Mixing metals

We often use metals on their own for jobs. For example, we make some cooking pans from copper. Copper dents and bends easily. We can improve the **properties** of metals by mixing them with other metals or substances. These new metals are called **alloys**. For example, nickel is added to copper to make copper harder. We use this alloy to make coins.

This doorknob is made from brass, an alloy of copper and zinc.

Steel is the metal we use most. Steel is not a pure metal. It is an alloy. It is made by mixing a tiny amount of carbon, which is not a metal, with **molten** iron. A thin rod of pure iron is soft and easy to bend. Steel is much harder and stronger than pure iron. We use steel in buildings, ships, car bodies and machine parts.

Don't use it!

Some alloys are very expensive to make because they contain metals that are hard to find. We don't use these alloys, or rare metals such as platinum, to make everyday objects such as drain covers and cutlery that don't need special properties. We use cheap metals such as iron and steel for these jobs instead.

Metals, water and air

If an object made from iron or **steel** gets damp, it will quickly turn brown. The brown substance is called rust. If the metal stays damp, it will gradually be eaten away by rust and turn weak and crumbly. Rusting is an example of a process called corrosion. Other metals **corrode** when they get damp, too. Some metals, such as gold and titanium, do not corrode at all.

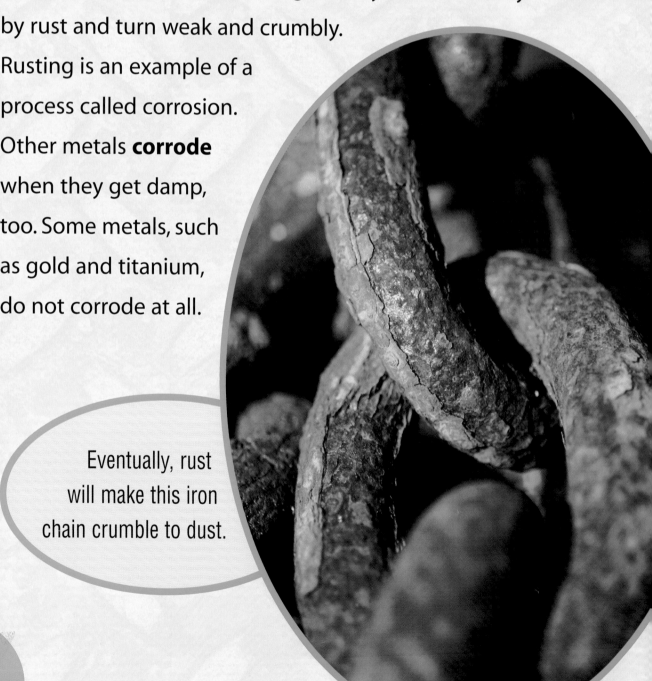

Eventually, rust will make this iron chain crumble to dust.

Steel cans are coated with tin to stop them rusting.

Rust makes things weak so it is important to stop it happening. One way to prevent rusting is to stop water reaching it. We can do this by covering the surface of the metal with oil or paint. We can also cover it with a layer of a metal that does not rust, such as zinc or chrome. A special sort of steel called stainless steel does not rust. It is an **alloy** of steel, nickel and chromium. We use it to make sinks, cutlery and worktops.

Don't use it!

For some jobs we cannot use metals that corrode. For example, a replacement hip joint made of metal must not corrode inside a person's body. We use metals that don't corrode instead, such as titanium.

Metals for decoration

All metals are shiny when they are freshly cut and polished. They also come in different colours. For example, aluminium is shiny and grey. Brass is shiny and yellow. We use the shine and colour of metals for decoration. For example, we make ornaments from brass and light fittings from aluminium.

This light fitting is made from polished metal.

These medals were awarded for bravery in wartime.

Jewellery can be made from gold or silver. These metals have a beautiful colour and are very shiny. They are also soft metals that are easy to cut and shape into delicate jewellery. Some jewellery is made of a cheaper metal, such as brass, with a thin coat of gold or silver on top. This is called gold plate or silver plate.

Don't use it!

*We don't use metals that **corrode**, such as iron, to make jewellery. It rusts easily and does not look shiny. However, some sculptures are made from copper because it turns green as it corrodes.*

Metals and the environment

Throwing metals away can cause problems for the environment. Metals do not rot away quickly like some other materials such as wood. Rusting cars, food cans and other metals fill up rubbish dumps and can harm animals and people. Some metals are very poisonous. Mercury is the only metal that is a **liquid** at room **temperature**. We use it for many jobs. However, it can poison fish and people if it gets into rivers.

An abandoned car can take years to rust away.

These aluminium drinks cans are waiting to be recycled.

Metals such as **steel**, aluminium and gold can be **recycled**. We can melt objects made from these metals and make them into new objects. Recycling metals is good for the environment. Mining and **smelting** metals uses huge amounts of **energy**, which comes from burning fuels. If we recycle metals we save this energy and the pollution it causes. Recycling also saves digging up the ground for more **ores**, and can save habitats where plants and animals live.

Find out for yourself

The best way to find out more about metals is to investigate them for yourself. Look around your home for things made from metal, and keep an eye out for metal during your day. Think about why metal was used for each job. What properties make it suitable? You will find the answers to many of your questions in this book. You can also look in other books and on the Internet.

Books to read

Science Answers: Grouping Materials, Carol Ballard, (Heinemann Library, 2003)

Discovering Science: Matter, Rebecca Hunter (Raintree, 2003)

Find Out About Metal, Henry Pluckrose (Franklin Watts, 2002)

Using the Internet

Try searching the Internet to find out about metal. Websites can change, so if some of the links below no longer work, don't worry. Use a search engine such as www.yahooligans.com or www.internet4kids.com. You could try searching using the keywords 'iron smelting', 'copper' and 'supermagnet'. Here are some websites to get you started.

Websites

A great site, which explains all about different materials:
http://www.bbc.co.uk/schools/revisewise/science/materials/

Help for science projects and homework, and free science clip art:
http://schools.discovery.com/students

Disclaimer
All the internet addresses (URLs) given in this book were valid at the time of going to press. However, due to the dynamic nature of the Internet, some addresses may have changed, or sites may have ceased to exist since publication. While the author and publishers regret any inconvenience this may cause readers, no responsibility for any such changes can be accepted by either the author or the publishers.

Glossary

alloy material made from two or more metals or a metal and another material

beam horizontal piece of a frame, supported at each end

chemical substance that we use to make other substances, or for jobs such as cleaning

circuit boards set of wires that are designed to carry electricity for a particular purpose

coke fuel made by heating coal

column vertical piece of a frame

concrete material made from cement and gravel

conduct carry or transmit heat or electricity

corrode be slowly eaten away

crust layer of solid rock that forms the outer layer of the Earth

dynamo device that makes electricity when it is spun round

elastic able to stretch and return to its original shape

electromagnet iron bar, around which wire is coiled, that becomes a magnet when electricity flows through the wire

energy power to do work

limestone type of rock

liquid something in a runny state that can be poured from one container to another

magnet material that attracts iron

molten melted

natural anything that is not made by people

ore rock that we get metals from

property characteristic or quality of a material

raw material material that we get other materials from or that we make into other materials

rechargeable battery that we can put electricity back into after using it

recycle use again

smelting process of getting metals from their ores

solid having a fixed shape and size

steel alloy of iron and carbon

temperature measure of how hot or cold something is

Index

Titles in the *Using Materials* series include:

Hardback   1 844 43436 2

Hardback   1 844 43437 0

Hardback   1 844 43438 9

Hardback   1 844 43439 7

Hardback   1 844 43440 0

Hardback   1 844 43441 9

Find out about the other titles in this series on our website www.raintreepublishers.co.uk